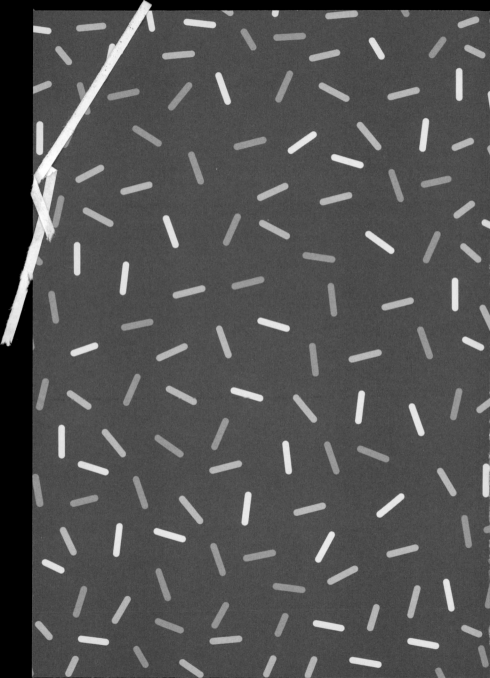

Donut Grow Up

(IT'S A TRAP)

circus

An Hachette UK Company
www.hachette.co.uk

Circus Books, an imprint of Summersdale Publishers Ltd
Part of Octopus Publishing Group Limited
Carmelite House
50 Victoria Embankment
LONDON
EC4Y 0DZ
UK

www.summersdale.com

Printed and bound in China

ISBN: 978-1-78783-220-6

Substantial discounts on bulk quantities of Summersdale books are available to corporations, professional associations and other organizations. For details contact general enquiries: telephone: +44 (0) 1243 771107 or email: enquiries@summersdale.com.

10 9 8 7 6 5 4 3 2 1

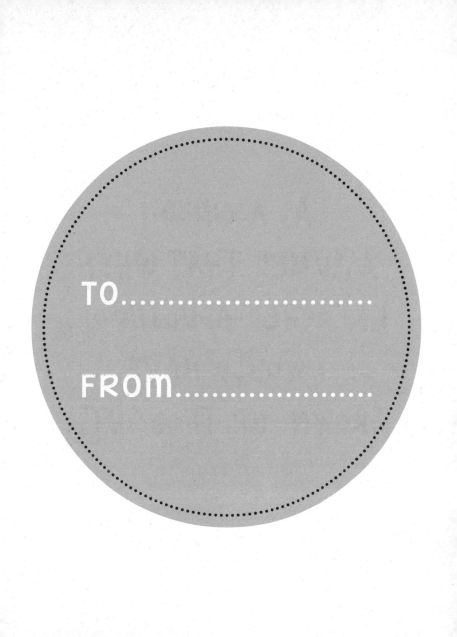

TO.........................

FROM....................

AS A CHILD I
ASSUMED THAT WHEN
I REACHED ADULTHOOD,
I WOULD HAVE
GROWN-UP THOUGHTS.

David Sedaris

There's power
in looking silly
and not caring
that you do.

AMY POEHLER

ADULT-
IN-TRAINING

Too much of a
good thing can
be wonderful.

MAE WEST

MIX A LITTLE FOOLISHNESS WITH YOUR SERIOUS PLANS. IT IS LOVELY TO BE SILLY AT THE RIGHT MOMENT.

HORACE

MY CHILDHOOD MAY
BE OVER BUT THAT
DOESN'T MEAN
PLAYTIME IS.

Ronald Olson

Life's a party

(SO WHERE'S MY GOODY BAG?)

I BELIEVE THAT
EVERYONE ELSE MY
AGE IS AN ADULT
WHEREAS I AM
MERELY IN DISGUISE.

Margaret Atwood

THE TRICK IS
GROWING UP
WITHOUT
GROWING OLD.

Casey Stengel

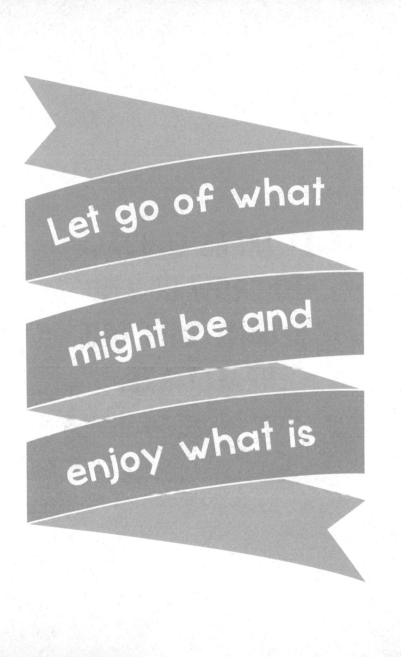

IT TAKES COURAGE TO GROW UP AND BECOME WHO YOU REALLY ARE.

E. E. Cummings

Be yourself.
The world worships
the original.

INGRID BERGMAN

YOU THINK THAT
ADULTHOOD WILL HIT
AND YOU'LL SUDDENLY
BE MORE CAPABLE. BUT
THAT DOESN'T HAPPEN,
EVER, DOES IT?

Sally Hawkins

LIFE'S MORE INTERESTING WHEN YOU COLOR OUTSIDE THE LINES

ADULTS ARE ALWAYS
ASKING LITTLE KIDS
WHAT THEY WANT TO
BE WHEN THEY GROW
UP BECAUSE THEY'RE
LOOKING FOR IDEAS.

Paula Poundstone

**Trust in dreams,
for in them is hidden
the gate to eternity.**

KAHLIL GIBRAN

I'M FLYING
OFF TO
NEVERLAND

When we are
children we seldom
think of the future.
This innocence
leaves us free to
enjoy ourselves as
few adults can.

PATRICK ROTHFUSS

EMBRACE THE GLORIOUS MESS THAT YOU ARE.

ELIZABETH GILBERT

EVEN THOUGH
YOU'RE GROWING UP,
YOU SHOULD NEVER
STOP HAVING FUN.

Nina Dobrev

WHAT A DISTRESSING
CONTRAST THERE IS
BETWEEN THE RADIANT
INTELLIGENCE OF THE
CHILD AND THE FEEBLE
MENTALITY OF THE
AVERAGE ADULT.

Sigmund Freud

GROWING UP IS SUCH A BARBAROUS BUSINESS, FULL OF INCONVENIENCE AND PIMPLES.

J. M. Barrie

Stay young and fun

(AND MARCH TO THE BEAT
OF YOUR OWN DRUM)

May you live
all the days
of your life.

JONATHAN SWIFT

A CHILD BECOMES
AN ADULT WHEN HE
REALIZES THAT HE HAS
A RIGHT NOT ONLY TO
BE RIGHT BUT ALSO
TO BE WRONG.

Thomas Szasz

JUST WHEN THE CATERPILLAR THOUGHT THE WORLD WAS OVER, IT BECAME A BUTTERFLY.

ANONYMOUS

I'm not going to be an adult, I'm going to be a bigger child

THE GREAT THING IN
THIS WORLD IS NOT SO
MUCH WHERE WE STAND,
AS IN WHAT DIRECTION
WE ARE MOVING.

Oliver Wendell Holmes

The key
to successful
ageing is to pay
as little attention
to it as possible.

JUDITH REGAN

ALWAYS CHOOSE
THE SCENIC
ROUTE

That's the real trouble with the world, too many people grow up.

WALT DISNEY

BE NOT AFRAID OF LIFE.

BELIEVE THAT LIFE IS WORTH LIVING, AND YOUR BELIEF WILL HELP CREATE THE FACT.

WILLIAM JAMES

YOU'RE ONLY YOUNG
ONCE, BUT YOU CAN BE
IMMATURE FOREVER.

Germaine Greer

LAUGHTER IS THE
BRUSH THAT SWEEPS
AWAY THE COBWEBS
OF YOUR HEART.

Mort Walker

SOME DAY YOU WILL BE OLD ENOUGH TO START READING FAIRY TALES AGAIN.

C. S. Lewis

ADULTHOOD REQUIRES 100% MORE GLITTER

A HEAD FULL OF DREAMS HAS NO SPACE FOR FEARS.

Anonymous

☆

Life just happens – enjoy it anyway.

JONATHAN LOCKWOOD HUIE

LIVE AS IF YOU WERE
TO DIE TOMORROW.
LEARN AS IF YOU WERE
TO LIVE FOREVER.

Anonymous

You can
be anything
you want
to be

(SO BE A UNICORN)

What is an adult?
A child blown
up by age.

SIMONE DE BEAUVOIR

The world only
exists in your eyes.
You can make it as
big or as small
as you want.

F. SCOTT FITZGERALD

I'M A HUMAN MACHINE POWERED BY IMAGINATION

NOT ALL
THOSE WHO
WANDER
ARE LOST.

J. R. R. TOLKIEN

LIFE ISN'T ABOUT FINDING
YOURSELF; IT'S ABOUT
CREATING YOURSELF.

George Bernard Shaw

IT IS MORE FUN
TO BE THE PAINTER
THAN THE PAINT.

George Clooney

GROWING OLD IS MANDATORY. GROWING UP IS OPTIONAL.

Chili Davis

You are
never too old
to set another
goal or to
dream a
new dream.

LES BROWN

The older
you get the
more you realize
that nobody else
knows what's
going on
either

THIS LIFE IS WHAT YOU MAKE IT.

Marilyn Monroe

Don't count
the days;
make the
days count.

MUHAMMAD ALI

IF YOU WAIT,
ALL THAT HAPPENS
IS THAT YOU
GET OLDER.

Mario Andretti

DOWN WITH ADULTING, UP WITH KIDULTING!

EVERYONE THINKS YOU MAKE MISTAKES WHEN YOU'RE YOUNG. BUT I DON'T THINK WE MAKE ANY FEWER WHEN WE'RE GROWN UP.

JODI PICOULT

LIFE IS A GREAT BIG
CANVAS, AND YOU
SHOULD THROW ALL
THE PAINT ON
IT YOU CAN.

Danny Kaye

Don't be jelly

(BE NICE CREAM)

YOU'RE PERFECT WHEN
YOU'RE COMFORTABLE
BEING YOURSELF.

Ansel Elgort

WE LIVE IN DEEDS, NOT YEARS; IN THOUGHTS, NOT BREATHS; IN FEELINGS, NOT IN FIGURES ON A DIAL.

Philip James Bailey

Even if you
fall on your
face, you're still
moving forward.

VICTOR KIAM

DO A CARTWHEEL EVERY DAY

ONE WAY TO GET THE
MOST OUT OF LIFE IS
TO LOOK UPON IT AS
AN ADVENTURE.

William Feather

LIFE IS TO BE ENJOYED, NOT JUST ENDURED.

Gordon B. Hinckley

HAPPINESS
IS A KIND
OF MAGIC

Look at everything always as though you were seeing it either for the first or last time.

BETTY SMITH

Your attitude is like a
box of crayons that
color your world.

ALLEN KLEIN

MEN DO NOT QUIT
PLAYING BECAUSE
THEY GROW OLD; THEY
GROW OLD BECAUSE
THEY QUIT PLAYING.

Oliver Wendell Holmes Sr

EVERY DAY BRINGS A CHANCE FOR YOU TO DRAW IN A BREATH, KICK OFF YOUR SHOES... AND DANCE.

OPRAH WINFREY

PEOPLE NEVER GROW UP,
THEY JUST LEARN HOW
TO ACT IN PUBLIC.

Bryan White

Keep searching
for the end
of the rainbow

EVERY MORNING
IS A CHANCE AT
A NEW DAY.

Marjorie Pay Hinckley

All life is
an experiment.
The more
experiments
you make the
better.

RALPH WALDO EMERSON

YOU LIVE BUT ONCE; YOU MIGHT AS WELL BE AMUSING.

Coco Chanel

Hugs
solve
problems

(AND SO DO NAPS)

BE IN LOVE WITH
YOUR LIFE. EVERY
MINUTE OF IT.

Jack Kerouac

Don't go through life, grow through life.

ERIC BUTTERWORTH

SHH, DON'T TELL ANYONE BUT I'M MAKING THIS UP AS I GO ALONG!

I DON'T WANT OTHER PEOPLE TO DECIDE WHO I AM. I WANT TO DECIDE THAT FOR MYSELF.

EMMA WATSON

TO SUCCEED IN LIFE,
YOU NEED THREE THINGS:
A WISHBONE,
A BACKBONE AND
A FUNNY BONE.

Reba McEntire

I PROMISE YOU THAT EACH AND EVERY ONE OF YOU IS MADE TO BE WHO YOU ARE.

Selena Gomez

Believe in

fairies, mermaids

and wishes

EXPLORE,
DREAM,
DISCOVER.

H. Jackson Brown Jr

It is only possible
to live happily ever
after on a day-
to-day basis.

MARGARET BONANNO

HELP!
PEOPLE ARE
MISTAKING
ME FOR A
GROWN-UP!

TRADITION WEARS
A SNOWY BEARD,
ROMANCE IS
ALWAYS YOUNG.

John Greenleaf Whittier

NOTHING GREAT WAS EVER ACHIEVED WITHOUT ENTHUSIASM.

Ralph Waldo Emerson

Do what you can,
with what you've got,
where you are.

WILLIAM WIDENER

I PUSH DOORS THAT SAY "PULL"

I don't know
where I'm going
from here but I
promise it won't
be boring.

DAVID BOWIE

I HAVE FOUND THAT IF YOU LOVE LIFE, LIFE WILL LOVE YOU BACK.

ARTHUR RUBINSTEIN

Do things that feel good

(LIKE BIKE RIDES
AND KISSES)

FIND OUT WHO YOU ARE
AND BE THAT PERSON...
FIND THAT TRUTH,
LIVE THAT TRUTH
AND EVERYTHING
ELSE WILL COME.

Ellen DeGeneres

IT'S JUST LIFE.
JUST LIVE IT.

Terri Guillemets

PLUNGE BOLDLY INTO THE THICK OF LIFE, AND SEIZE IT WHERE YOU WILL, IT IS ALWAYS INTERESTING.

Johann Wolfgang von Goethe

Stay strong
and be yourself!
It's the best thing
you can be.

CARA DELEVINGNE

MATURITY IS A
HIGH PRICE TO PAY
FOR GROWING UP.

Tom Stoppard

Life feels
like an exam
I didn't
revise for

BEING SILLY IS STILL ALLOWED, NOT EXCLUDED BY ADULTHOOD! WHAT'S EXCLUDED BY ADULTHOOD IS THOUGHTLESSNESS, SO BE THOUGHTFUL AND SILLY.

Hank Green

What if we
just pretended
like everything
was easy?

MARY ANNE RADMACHER

IT TAKES A LONG TIME
TO BECOME YOUNG.

Pablo Picasso

HAPPINESS IS NOT HAVING TO SET THE ALARM FOR THE NEXT DAY

GO CONFIDENTLY IN THE DIRECTION OF YOUR DREAMS! LIVE THE LIFE YOU'VE IMAGINED.

HENRY DAVID THOREAU

TO BE OLD AND
WISE YOU MUST
FIRST BE YOUNG
AND FOOLISH.

Anonymous

A HEART THAT LOVES IS ALWAYS YOUNG.

Greek proverb

Dare to
love yourself
as if you were
a rainbow
with gold at
both ends.

ABERJHANI

ALL WOULD
LIVE LONG, BUT NONE
WOULD BE OLD.

Benjamin Franklin

Every day may not be good

(BUT THERE'S GOOD IN EVERY DAY)

I spent my whole childhood wishing I were older and now I'm spending my adulthood wishing I were younger.

RICKY SCHRODER

The scariest moment
is always just
before you start.

STEPHEN KING

DO SOMETHING NEW EVERY DAY

IT'S NEVER TOO LATE
TO TAKE A LEAP OF
FAITH AND SEE WHAT
WILL HAPPEN –
AND TO BE
BRAVE IN LIFE.

Jane Fonda

LIFE MOVES ON AND SO SHOULD WE.

Spencer Johnson

LIFE IS EITHER A DARING ADVENTURE OR NOTHING.

Helen Keller

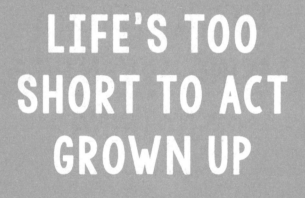

LIFE'S TOO
SHORT TO ACT
GROWN UP

GREATNESS IS MORE THAN POTENTIAL. IT IS THE EXECUTION OF THAT POTENTIAL.

ERIC BURNS

THE TRICK IS TO ENJOY LIFE. DON'T WISH AWAY YOUR DAYS, WAITING FOR BETTER ONES AHEAD.

Marjorie Pay Hinckley

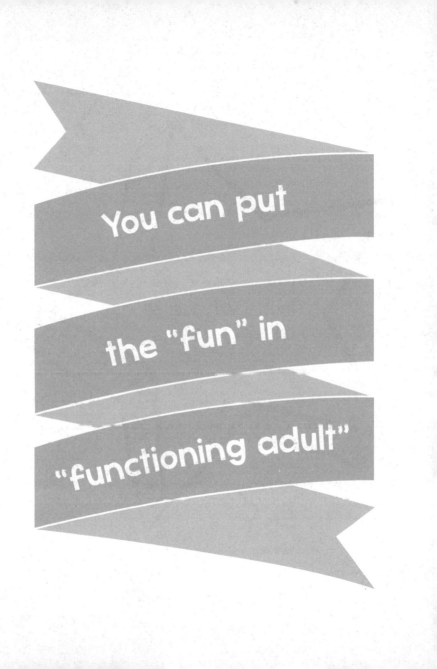

Those who love deeply never grow old.

ARTHUR WING PINERO

MATURITY CONSISTS IN
HAVING REDISCOVERED
THE SERIOUSNESS
ONE HAD AS A
CHILD AT PLAY.

Friedrich Nietzsche

DIFFICULT ROADS
OFTEN LEAD
TO BEAUTIFUL
DESTINATIONS.

Zig Ziglar

There are good days and then there are days when I put my coat on backwards

NOTHING REALLY MATTERS EXCEPT WHAT YOU DO NOW IN THIS INSTANT OF TIME.

Eileen Caddy

If we were meant to stay in one place, we'd have roots instead of feet.

RACHEL WOLCHIN

Your
time as a
caterpillar
has expired

(YOUR WINGS ARE READY)

Set your goals high,
and don't stop till
you get there.

BO JACKSON

ADULTS ARE JUST OBSOLETE CHILDREN AND THE HELL WITH THEM.

DR SEUSS

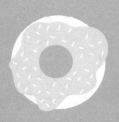

EITHER YOU
RUN THE DAY OR
THE DAY RUNS YOU.

Jim Rohn

GROWING UP HAPPENS
WHEN YOU START
HAVING THINGS
YOU LOOK BACK
ON AND WISH YOU
COULD CHANGE.

Cassandra Clare

NOTHING IS
A WASTE OF TIME
IF YOU USE THE
EXPERIENCE WISELY.

Auguste Rodin

I'M STILL WAITING FOR THE WISDOM THAT SUPPOSEDLY COMES WITH AGE

BE GLAD OF LIFE BECAUSE IT GIVES YOU THE CHANCE TO LOVE, TO WORK, TO PLAY AND TO LOOK UP AT THE STARS.

Henry van Dyke

Begin to be now
what you will
be hereafter.

WILLIAM JAMES

Laughing makes everything easier.

CARMEN ELECTRA

Wherever
you are, be
all there.

JIM ELLIOT

IN MY CASE,
ADULTHOOD ITSELF
WAS NOT AN ADVANCE,
ALTHOUGH IT WAS A
USEFUL WAYMARK.

Nicholson Baker

A boy becomes an adult
three years before his
parents think he does,
and about two years
after he thinks he does.

LEWIS HERSHEY

TELL ME,
WHAT IS IT YOU
PLAN TO DO WITH
YOUR ONE WILD AND
PRECIOUS LIFE?

Mary Oliver

WHEN ASKED IF MY CUP IS HALF-FULL OR HALF-EMPTY MY ONLY RESPONSE IS THAT I AM THANKFUL I HAVE A CUP.

SAM LEFKOWITZ

EVERY DAY BRINGS NEW CHOICES.

Martha Beck

It's OK to stay in the comfort zone

(THERE ARE
BEANBAGS THERE)

TURN YOUR FACE TO THE SUN AND THE SHADOWS FALL BEHIND YOU.

Maori proverb

Growing up
is losing some
illusions, in order
to acquire others.

VIRGINIA WOOLF

DON'T WASTE YOUR YOUTH TRYING TO GROW UP

YOU ONLY LIVE ONCE, BUT IF YOU DO IT RIGHT, ONCE IS ENOUGH.

MAE WEST

IF NOT NOW, WHEN?

WHEN?

Hillel the Elder

LOOK AT LIFE
THROUGH THE
WINDSHIELD,
NOT THE
REAR-VIEW
MIRROR.

Byrd Baggett

LIVE EACH DAY AS IF YOUR LIFE HAD JUST BEGUN.

Johann Wolfgang von Goethe

DON'T GROW UP; IT'S A TRAP!

If you're interested in finding out more about our books, find us on Facebook at Summersdale Publishers **and follow us on Twitter at** @Summersdale

www.summersdale.com

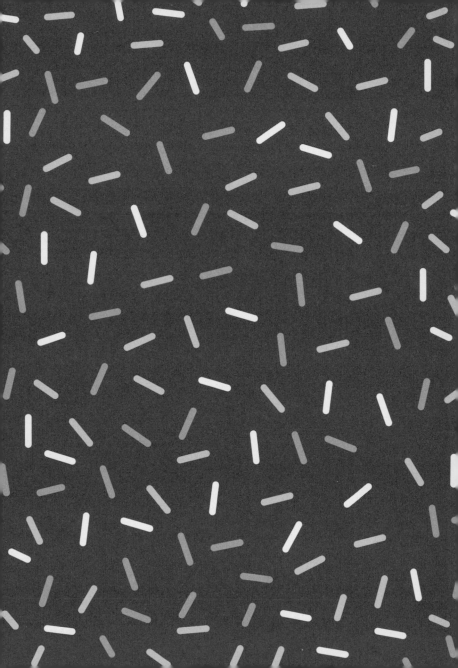